THE CHORUS OF THE SOUL

LEHLOHONOLO PHINEAS LEBESA

Made with ❤ on the Notion Press Platform
www.notionpress.com

To the nights spent staring at a blanc page, the days spent
searching for inpiration , and the years spent honoring my craft-
this book is for all writers out there who never give up their
passion . To my family, who always believed in my deams and
encouraged me to write.

Contents

Contents

Foreword

Poetry has been a lifelong passion of mine. Its a way I make sense of the world, and the way I express my thoughts and feelings.

Preface

Poem is a form of expression that has been with us for centuries, and its appeal has endured through ages. It has been used to convey powerful emotions, tell stories and explore philosophical ideas. I hope that this poems will resonate with readers and offer glimps of human experience.

Acknowledgements

I would like to thank my loving and supportive family for their unwavering support and encouragement .

Prologue

As a child, I always loved poetry. It was my first time when I felt like I had found my own voice. I found through poetry, my own voice. I found that through poetry, I could express my deepest feeings and thoughts in a way that I was uniquely my own. As a teen, I am still drawn to the power of poetry to convey the human experience. In this collection, I have tried to capture a range of emotions, from joy to love to grief and loss.

THE GREAT PAUSE

In times of darkness, a tale unfolds,
Of a pandemic we now behold,
COVID-19, it came to spread,
A storm that filled us with dread.

It started small, a whisper in the air,
A virus unknown, caught us unaware,
From distant lands, it swiftly came,
With every touch and every name.

Across the globe, it travelled fast,
No country untouched by its vast,
From city streets to quiet towns,
It left its mark, it wore its crowns.

Lockdowns enforced, we stood apart,
Aching for connection, with heavy hearts,
No more embraces, no more laughter,
The world grew still, and silence after.

Struggling doctors, nurses, heroes true,
Fighting battles they never knew,
Putting their lives on the front line,
To care for patients, time after time.

Schools closed down, Students stayed home,
Learning through screens, in rooms they roamed,
Parents became teachers, day by day,
Navigating a new world, finding their way.

Businesses shuttered, people in need,
Jobs lost, dreams crushed, like a broken seed,
But through the darkness, a light did gleam,
A spirit of resilience, a hopeful dream.

Communities united, lending a hand,
Neighbours helping neighbours, across the land,
Front porches filled with cheers and claps,
For essential workers, who bridged the gaps.

Virtual hugs and Zoom-filled nights,
Love transmitted through digital lights,
Though physically apart, we found a way,
To connect our hearts, each and every day.

Scientists raced against the clock,
Searching for answers around the clock,
A vaccine promised, a glimmer of hope,
To bring an end to this pandemic's scope.

And as we journeyed through these trials,
We discovered strength in our smiles,
COVID-19 may have knocked us down,
But it won't defeat us, we'll wear our crown.

For in our hearts, a flame still burns,
Together we stand, as the world turns,
With hope and love, we'll rise above,
This pandemic, united, with unwavering love.

THE QUEST FOR CURES

In the realm of medicine through time,
Where knowledge meets substances so prime,
Pharmaceutical Sciences, a field profound,
Unravelling mysteries, where cures are found.

In labs they dwell, the curious minds,
Seeking answers, where science binds,
Chemical concoctions, molecules abound,
To heal the sick, in each compound.

Drug research, their noble quest,
To find the treatments that are best,
From ancient herbs to synthetic blends,
Unlocking secrets that nature sends.

They study drugs, their effects and more,
From their creation to the drugstore,
Analysing properties, understanding the way,
To heal ailments that come our way.

They delve into the biochemistry,
Understanding the human body's mystery,
How drugs interact, in complex ways,
To mend our cells, and grant brighter days.

In pharmacology, a world unfolds,
Testing drugs, as stories are told,
Lab animals, their health a guide,
To ensure the treatments coincide.

Clinical trials, a significant stage,
Testing drugs on humans, page by page,
To determine their efficacy,
And study side effects with accuracy.

Pharmacokinetics, they delve into,
Understanding how drugs break through,
Absorption, distribution, and metabolism too,
Excretion, the journey each drug must pursue.

From drug design to formulation's art,
Finding ways to heal ailing hearts,
Drug delivery systems, innovation's stride,
Enhancing efficacy, with each new ride.

Pharmaceutical Sciences, a tapestry vast,
Bringing hope to lives, with knowledge amassed,
With every breakthrough the human race,
Find solace in their embrace.

So, honour the researchers, the science embraced,

The discoveries made, in each case,

For their work impacts lives, day by day,

As they pave the path for a healthier way.

In the realm of Pharmaceutical Sciences,

Where research and healing dances,

Endlessly pursuing a brighter dawn,

With each new drug, a victory is drawn.

THE GREAT ADVENTURE

From the moment of conception, in a mother's womb,
Life begins, a journey of growth to bloom.
A tiny seed, hidden in the depths of creation,
Slowly evolving, a miraculous manifestation.

The cells divide, multiplying in rapid pace,
Forming the foundation of beauty and grace.
From a single cell, a complex web unfurls,
The miracle of life, as nature joyously swirls.

As days turn to weeks, a heartbeat is heard,
A rhythm of life, like a sweet song preferred.
Organs take shape, developing with care,
Nurtured by love, in a tender embrace fair.

Limbs sprout and grow, reaching for the sky,
Delicate fingers and toes, like wings to fly.
Forming a body, a vessel for the soul,
A masterpiece in progress, a wondrous goal.

From a tiny foetus, nestled and secure,
To a newborn babe, the world to explore.
With every breath, a burst of life's song,
Growing and learning, the journey is long.

Infancy embraces with cuddles and coos,
A time of pure innocence, where love accrues.
Discovering the world, through curious eyes,
The wonder and awe, as each day arises.

The toddler years, a dance of wobbly steps,
Embarking on a path, where independence creeps in.
Falling and stumbling, learning to rise,
Life lessons etched, in every stumble and try.

The child emerges, a sponge to absorb,
Knowledge and wisdom, their minds explore.
From their first words to their first learned letter,
A thirst for learning, a drive that will never fetter.

Adolescence blooms, like a flower in spring,
Awakening passions, where dreams take wing.
Navigating through new emotions and change,
Finding their place, a life rearranged.

With adulthood's arrival, responsibilities call,
Choices are made, as life's path befalls.
Education and career, a purpose to fulfil,
Building foundations, on the journey uphill.

Through love and laughter, heartaches and pain,
The human spirit grows, never in vain.

Relationships formed, bonds that withstand,
Nurturing souls, holding each other's hand.

Midlife's wisdom, a wellspring of grace,
Reflecting on memories, life's winning embrace.
Lessons learned, from joys and mistakes,
Navigating challenges, till the spirit awakes.

And as the sun sets, towards the elder years,
A lifetime of experiences, laughter, and tears.
Wrinkles and grey hairs, hold tales untold,
A reservoir of wisdom, a heart made bold.

With each passing year, a beautiful bloom,
Enveloped in love, dispelling any gloom.
A life well-lived, from foetus to elder,
Reminding us to cherish, every fleeting hour.

So, let us celebrate the growth of the human being,
From the miracle of birth, to a life well-seeing.
In each phase and stage, let love be our guide,
For the growth of the human spirit, forever by our side.

THE CRADLE OF CIVILIZATION

In Africa, a land so grand,
Nature's masterpiece, this enchanting land,
From vast savannahs to towering peaks,
A tapestry of wonders that truly speaks.

From the Sahara's golden dunes,
To the cascading Victoria Falls, nature's tunes,
Africa, a continent of diverse faces,
A treasure trove of cultures and vibrant spaces.

In the Serengeti's endless plains,
Where the lion roams and the wildebeest trains,
A symphony of wildlife, untamed and free,
In this untamed land, such beauty we see.

Mount Kilimanjaro, reaching into the skies,
A majestic peak, where dreams arise,
Crowned with snow, a sight so rare,
Africa's grandeur, in the crisp mountain air.

The Nile, a lifeline coursing through,
A ribbon of life, where ancient civilizations grew,
Along its banks, stories are told,

Of kings and queens, and legends bold.

From Morocco's labyrinthine souks,
To Egypt's pyramids, standing in cloaks,
Africa's history, long and deep,
Its ancient tales, in whispers, seep.

Ghana's vibrant markets, a cacophony of sound,
Colours abound, traditions profound,
Nigeria's bustling cities, pulsating with life,
A cultural fusion, where diversity thrives.

Rainforests, a lush green canopy,
Harbouring mysteries, for all to see,
The great Congo Basin, a haven for life,
Gorillas and elephants, amidst the strife.

Lesotho, the Kingdom In the Sky,
the well of hospitality, land of mountains tall,
With colours vibrant, red, green blue,
The sunsets here, what else can do?
Your beauty cannot be matched.

South Africa's cape, where oceans meet,
With penguins waddling to greet,
One can witness the Big Five reign,
In Kruger Park, their majestic domain.

Africa, a continent with a beating heart,
The rhythm of life, where moments start,
The warmth of its people, a radiant glow,
Welcoming smiles, wherever you go.

But Africa's story is not without pain,
Colonial scars, still leaving a stain,
Yet strength prevails, resilience stands,
United together, holding hands.

Africa, a land of vast potential,
Harnessing innovation, becoming essential,
Rising above challenges, reaching for the sky,
A continent on the verge, ready to fly.

In Africa, a land so grand,
Nature's masterpiece, where wonders expand,
Rich in its heritage, bold and bright,
Africa's spirit shines, with timeless might.

THE WORLD ENGINE

The World Engine

In a world of change and innovation,
Where the wheels of progress are in motion,
There's a revolution birthing in sight,
Spanning continents, by day and night.

It starts with industrialization bold,
Machines woven into every fabric and fold,
The clang of gears, the rhythmic hum,
Transforming landscapes, where once was calm.

Factories rise like towering giants,
Breathing fire, fueling desires,
Unleashing the power of technology,
Shaping our world's new geography.

Robots emerge, with precision and grace,
Moving swiftly, filling any space,
Their metal hearts beat with endless might,
A symphony of AI, glowing bright.

They toil and labour, tireless as can be,
Freeing humans from drudgery,
Automation dances, a melody divine,

Whispering promises of a future benign.

Yet amidst the progress, questions arise,
Will robots replace human guise?
What of those whose labour they displace,
How to ensure a fair and just embrace?

But progress waits for no one's demand,
A force that surpasses the human hand,
It's up to us to keep evolving our gaze,
Uncover paths for balanced days.

For in this world of machines and code,
We find opportunities to lighten our load,
To redefine our roles, to adapt and mend,
Harnessing the power of our minds, to transcend.

So let us embrace this industrial tide,
With open minds and hearts beside,
For a revolution of world and soul,
Unfolds, as the wheels of change never cease to roll.

THE PATH OF ENLIGHTENMENT

The Path of Enlightenment

In the realm of knowledge, let us rejoice,
For education's gift is our soul's voice.
In simple words, this poem shall unfold,
The power of learning, shining like gold.

Come, gather round, and let me take you there,
To a world of wisdom, where minds are aware.
From the roots of curiosity, let's begin,
A journey of enlightenment, deep within.

Education, a spark that lights up the dark,
A beacon of hope, leaving no one stark.
It paves the way for dreams to come alive,
Empowering individuals to truly thrive.

In classrooms bright, young minds do ignite,
Igniting the fire, burning ever so bright.
Teachers, like stars, guide every step,
Nurturing spirits, never letting them forget.

From alphabets to numbers, the fundamentals start,
Building blocks of knowledge, an essential part.
Reading and writing, like wings to fly high,
Opening doors of perception, expanding the sky.

History whispers tales of the past,
Unravelling secrets, making memories last.
From ancient civilizations to modern age,
Education's key unlocks wisdom's sage.

Science, a treasure trove, waits to explore,
Unveiling the wonders we cannot ignore.
From the depths of atoms to galaxies unknown,
Education unleashes a curious mind that's grown.

Mathematics, the language of patterns and lines,
Solving complexities, where harmony shines.
With every equation, a puzzle piece we reveal,
Education unveils the truths we can feel.

In art's colourful canvas, emotions unfold,
Education nurtures the stories untold.
Brushstrokes of imagination, music's sweet song,
Creativity unleashed, bursting strong.

On the field of sports, lessons are learned,
Teamwork and perseverance, foundations churned.

With every victory or loss, character thrives,
Education in athletics, where greatness derives.

But education reaches beyond four walls,
To the depths of compassion, where humanity calls.
Fostering empathy, building bridges to unite,
Education ignites hearts, like stars in the night.

In classrooms diverse, cultures embrace,
Celebrating differences, breaking barriers in grace.
Empathy blossoms, understanding takes flight,
Education instils acceptance, shining bright.

Yet, education is not just for the young,
Throughout our lives, its song is sung.
It moulds and shapes, continuously evolves,
Guiding us through life's intricate corridors.

For the love of learning, let us stand tall,
Embrace education, may it be for us all.
In the journey of knowledge, let's never cease,
For education is the path to inner peace.

So, let us cherish the gift we've been bestowed,
Simple English or complex, may it be sowed.
The power of education, forever profound,
Transforming lives, lifting us from the ground.

In this epic art, its message is clear,
Education is a treasure, so hold it dear.
Unlock its potential, open every door,
And let the world learn, forever more.

PROMISE OF NEW DAY

Promise of New day

In the early morn, when darkness fades away,
A gentle glow emerges, welcoming the day.
The world awakens, as the sky turns bright,
A splendid scene unfolds, a breathtaking sight.

The sun peeks over the horizon's crest,
Painting the sky in colours, the very best.
Shades of pink and orange slowly unfurl,
As golden rays dance and twirl.

The birds begin to sing, their melodies sweet,
As nature rises up on its wondrous feet.
The world is filled with a golden haze,
A tranquil moment, it leaves us in a daze.

The sleepy land, now bathed in light,
Shadows recede, like creatures of the night.
Dewdrops on leaves sparkle and gleam,
In this divine moment, all is serene.

The sun, like a painter with its radiant brush,
Colours the world with a gentle hush.
Majestic mountains and rolling hills,

Valleys and meadows, adorned with thrills.

The warmth of the sunlight reaches the ground,
Embracing the earth all around.
It breathes life into flowers, trees, and streams,
Igniting their beauty, like magical dreams.

As morning progresses, the world comes alive,
With each passing moment, the day will thrive.
Gentle breezes carry scents of blooming flowers,
Whispering secrets through serene hours.

The sky transforms into a boundless blue,
As daylight treads, the past night bids adieu.
A brand-new day, a fresh start to embrace,
Embracing every moment, every trace.

So, rise with the sun, let its rays inspire,
Fill your heart with hope, let your spirit aspire.
For every sunrise holds a promise anew,
To live, to love, to make your dreams come true.

The Celestial Wonder
In the early morn, when darkness fades away,
A gentle glow emerges, welcoming the day.
The world awakens, as the sky turns bright,

A splendid scene unfolds, a breathtaking sight.

The sun peeks over the horizon's crest,
Painting the sky in colours, the very best.
Shades of pink and orange slowly unfurl,
As golden rays dance and twirl.

The birds begin to sing, their melodies sweet,
As nature rises up on its wondrous feet.
The world is filled with a golden haze,
A tranquil moment, it leaves us in a daze.

The sleepy land, now bathed in light,
Shadows recede, like creatures of the night.
Dewdrops on leaves sparkle and gleam,
In this divine moment, all is serene.

The sun, like a painter with its radiant brush,
Colours the world with a gentle hush.
Majestic mountains and rolling hills,
Valleys and meadows, adorned with thrills.

The warmth of the sunlight reaches the ground,
Embracing the earth all around.
It breathes life into flowers, trees, and streams,
Igniting their beauty, like magical dreams.

As morning progresses, the world comes alive,
With each passing moment, the day will thrive.
Gentle breezes carry scents of blooming flowers,
Whispering secrets through serene hours.

The sky transforms into a boundless blue,
As daylight treads, the past night bids adieu.
A brand-new day, a fresh start to embrace,
Embracing every moment, every trace.

So, rise with the sun, let its rays inspire,
Fill your heart with hope, let your spirit aspire.
For every sunrise holds a promise anew,
To live, to love, to make your dreams come true.

THE GLOBAL CHALLENGE

The Global Challenge

In a time when Earth's plight did unfold,
A tale of woe, of truths untold,
Climate change loomed, a fearsome beast,
Threatening our world from west to east.

The sky once painted a cerulean hue,
Now marred with grey, a sombre view,
The sun once warm, now scorching our land,
A blazing inferno where life can't withstand.

Oceans, once vibrant, teeming with life,
Now a graveyard of bleached coral strife,
Where majesties of the sea used to dwell,
Now plastic islands, a watery hell.

The polar ice caps, majestic and proud,
Crumbled and melted, no longer endowed,
With grandeur and beauty, a captivating sight,
Now drowning our shores, a sorrowful blight.

The seasons themselves, amiss and confused,
Springtime appears when winter is used,
Summer extends its burning embrace,

Autumn retreats, leaves betraying its grace.

Forests once lush, a tapestry of green,
Now withered, scorched, nowhere to be seen,
Devoured by flames, relentless and wild,
Ashes of hope, where serenity smiled.

Animals roam, bewildered and weak,
Their homes destroyed, refuge they seek,
Lost in the chaos, their numbers decline,
Extinction looms, a bitter, painful sign.

In this land of plenty, where greed has no bounds,
We poison the air with poisonous sounds,
Fumes and toxins invade every breath,
Choking our lungs, hastening death.

Yet in the face of this daunting plight,
There's still a glimmer of hope, shining bright,
For we are the guardians, summoned to act,
To heal our Earth, and counter the impact.

We must join hands, united as one,
An alliance of nations, till we are done,
Embrace renewable energy, embracing the sun,
Harnessing its power, a battle we've begun.

Educate the masses, spread awareness far and wide,
For apathy and ignorance we cannot abide,
Every choice matters, every action counts,
Together we'll rise, erasing our doubts.

Let's plant a forest, let nature reclaim,
Offer her solace, bring life to its frame,
Recycle, reduce, and refuse to consume,
It's time for real change, no longer assume.

For the sake of generations yet to come,
The future is at stake, the outcome not glum,
Climate change, the challenge we face,
Will we stand together, weaving a saving grace?

So, let this be a call to all,
To rise, to act, to never stall,
For Earth's existence, we hold the key,
To mend her wounds and set her free.

THE LAND OF DIVERSITY

The land of Diversity

In a time when Earth's plight did unfold,
A tale of woe, of truths untold,
Climate change loomed, a fearsome beast,
Threatening our world from west to east.

The sky once painted a cerulean hue,
Now marred with grey, a sombre view,
The sun once warm, now scorching our land,
A blazing inferno where life can't withstand.

Oceans, once vibrant, teeming with life,
Now a graveyard of bleached coral strife,
Where majesties of the sea used to dwell,
Now plastic islands, a watery hell.

The polar ice caps, majestic and proud,
Crumbled and melted, no longer endowed,
With grandeur and beauty, a captivating sight,
Now drowning our shores, a sorrowful blight.

The seasons themselves, amiss and confused,
Springtime appears when winter is used,
Summer extends its burning embrace,

Autumn retreats, leaves betraying its grace.

Forests once lush, a tapestry of green,
Now withered, scorched, nowhere to be seen,
Devoured by flames, relentless and wild,
Ashes of hope, where serenity smiled.

Animals roam, bewildered and weak,
Their homes destroyed, refuge they seek,
Lost in the chaos, their numbers decline,
Extinction looms, a bitter, painful sign.

In this land of plenty, where greed has no bounds,
We poison the air with poisonous sounds,
Fumes and toxins invade every breath,
Choking our lungs, hastening death.

Yet in the face of this daunting plight,
There's still a glimmer of hope, shining bright,
For we are the guardians, summoned to act,
To heal our Earth, and counter the impact.

We must join hands, united as one,
An alliance of nations, till we are done,
Embrace renewable energy, embracing the sun,
Harnessing its power, a battle we've begun.

Educate the masses, spread awareness far and wide,
For apathy and ignorance we cannot abide,
Every choice matters, every action counts,
Together we'll rise, erasing our doubts.

Let's plant a forest, let nature reclaim,
Offer her solace, bring life to its frame,
Recycle, reduce, and refuse to consume,
It's time for real change, no longer assume.

For the sake of generations yet to come,
The future is at stake, the outcome not glum,
Climate change, the challenge we face,
Will we stand together, weaving a saving grace?

So, let this be a call to all,
To rise, to act, to never stall,
For Earth's existence, we hold the key,
To mend her wounds and set her free.
In a land where wonders unfold,
History and culture, a story untold,
India, a land of vibrant hue,
A tapestry woven with sights anew.

From the northern peaks, mighty and grand,
To the southern shores, where coconuts stand,
From the eastern deltas, where rivers run deep,

To the western deserts, where camels leap.

In the heart of this ancient land,
A land where diversity boldly stands,
A billion souls, a tapestry of faces,
United by land, in diverse spaces.

From the sacred Ganges, flowing wide,
To the majestic Himalayas, reaching the sky,
India's landscape, a breathtaking sight,
With mountains and valleys, a wondrous height.

Rajasthan's deserts, a golden expanse,
Camels traverse, in a captivating dance,
Palaces and forts, telling tales of kings,
Courtyards and gardens, where history sings.

Amidst the chaos of city streets,
Mumbai's hustle, relentless beats,
A melting pot of cultures, blending as one,
Dreams and aspirations, under the sun.

In Kolkata, the City of Joy,
Intellect and artistry, they employ,
A tapestry of poets and vibrant souls,
Where passion and creativity truly unfolds.

In the south, where oceans embrace,
Kerala's backwaters, a tranquil space,
Tea plantations, vast and serene,
Tamil Nadu's temples, echoing the unseen.

A land of festivals, a riot of colours,
Holi's hues, Diwali's fervour,
Navratri's dance, Eid's feast,
Unity in diversity, a melody released.

The land where spirituality thrives,
Where the bells of temples and mosques chime,
Varanasi's ghats, where souls seek peace,
Harmony and faith, an eternal lease.

India, the home of great minds,
Rabindranath Tagore's words that bind,
Gandhi's teachings of peace and truth,
Lessons we learn, in our restless youth.

From Bollywood's silver screen delight,
To cuisine that enlivens every bite,
Spices dancing on our tongues,
Culture and flavours, perpetually sung.

But amidst the colours and tales so old,
India faces challenges untold,

Poverty's grip, a battle to fight,
Empowering minds, with all its might
Education, the key to unlock,
A brighter future, a pride that won't dock,
For every child deserves a chance,
To shine and rise, in life's grand dance.

So let us celebrate this Motherland,
Hold her close, lend her a helping hand,
India, land of wonders untold,
Imbued with stories, rich and bold.

THE MOUNTAIN KINGDOM

The mountain Kingdom

In the heart of southern Africa they say,
A land of beauty, where dreams hold sway,
Lesotho, my homeland, where I belong,
A land of mountains, where I grew strong.

Nestled high in the heavens above,
A kingdom of wonder, of hope and love,
Lesotho's peaks, mighty and tall,
Stretching their arms, protecting us all.

The Maloti Mountains, a glorious sight,
With blankets of snow, gleaming so bright,
Majestic and proud, they guard our land,
A symbol of resilience, sturdy and grand.

From Thaba-Bosiu's historic heights,
Where the echoes of history take flight,
Moshoeshoe, our father, a visionary king,
United our people, hope for his offering.

In the valleys below, where rivers flow,
Waterfalls cascade, a mesmerising show,
The Maletsunyane Falls, a majestic roar,
Captivating hearts, forevermore.

Through golden fields, dotted with herds,
Cattle graze peacefully, spreading words,
Of tradition and heritage, a way of life,
In harmony with nature, free from strife.

In the capital city, Maseru's embrace,
A vibrant rhythm, a bustling pace,
Where cultures converge, in joyful array,
Colours and sounds, a melodic display.

The Basotho people, resilient and true,
With kindness and warmth, they'll welcome you,
Their woven blankets, a cherished attire,
Embracing tradition, fueled by fire.

From the blankets to the iconic hats,
Symbolising strength, resilience, and that,
Lesotho, a nation, proud and kind,
Unwavering spirit, intertwined.

With each sunrise over the peaks so high,
Rural communities, where dreams amplify,

Schools and clinics, powered with hope,
Empowering young minds to soar and cope.

But Lesotho's spirit, forever bright,
Guides us through darkness, igniting light,
Together we strive, hand in hand,
Building a future, where dreams expand.

So, let this be a tribute to my land,
Lesotho, where I proudly stand,
A tapestry of mountains and plains,
Where I'll forever cherish its gentle reins.

THE LANGUAGE OF THE SOUL

In the realm of love, a wondrous terrain,
A tapestry of emotions, a heartfelt refrain,
There exist many types, as varied as can be,
Let me dive in, and help you see.

First, there's familial love, strong and pure,
A bond unbroken, forever secure,
From parents to siblings, a love so true,
Through thick and thin, they'll always see you through.

Then there's romantic love, a flame aflame,
Two souls entwined, sharing a name,
Passion ignites, in hearts that yearn,
Love's sweet dance, as the world turns.

Friendship blooms, another love so grand,
A companion in life, a helping hand,
Through laughter and tears, friendships grow,
Lifting spirits high, through highs and lows.

Self-love, a love often overlooked,
Nurturing oneself, feeling self-hooked,
For without love for oneself first and foremost,

Our love for others would be at its lowest.

Unconditional love, a love so rare,
No strings attached, no mask to wear,
A love that accepts, embraces flaws,
A love that uplifts, without any pause.

There's passionate love, filled with desire,
A fire that burns, unable to tire,
Intensity and fervour, hearts ablaze,
A love that consumes, in many ways.

Companionate love, a kind so calm,
A deep connection, a soothing balm,
Where friendship and affection intertwine,
A love that withstands the test of time.

Spiritual love, a love that transcends,
Connecting souls, where the divine extends,
A love for God, nature, or the universe,
Filling hearts with peace, comforting and diverse.

Puppy love, a young love so sweet,
Innocence and charm, a youthful beat,
Exploring feelings for the very first time,
A love that's tender, in its early prime.

Unrequited love, a bittersweet plight,
Feeling love's ache, in day and night,
Longing for someone, who's out of reach,
Yet cherishing the love, those words can't preach.

Love for humanity, in its grand scale,
A love that sees no borders, no land to trail,
A love that embraces, all colours and creeds,
A love that unites, fulfilling collective needs.

Maternal love, a love that's divine,
A mother's bond, forever in line,
Nurturing, protecting, with endless care,
A love that's unconditional, always there.

Paternal love, a father's embrace,
Guiding with strength, and steady grace,
A protector, a pillar, a guiding light,
A love that leads, both day and night.

Love for animals, a kindness so true,
A bond with creatures, that brings joy through,
A love that extends beyond our own kind,
Caring for those, with no voice to find.

In this vast spectrum of love's grand show,
Each type bears importance, that we must know,

For love is the essence, that makes us whole,
A universal language, to touch every soul.

So cherish the love, in all its form,
For it weathers life's storms, both cold and warm,
Let love be our anthem, shining so bright,
Guiding us forward, in love's eternal light.

THE FABRIC OF IDENTITY

In a world diverse, where nations unite,
Flags fly high, a symbol of their might,
Colours and emblems, waving in the air,
The pride of nations, to all who dare to stare.

Let's begin with the United States of America,
Old Glory's stars and stripes, a sight to remember,
Red, white, and blue, a beacon of liberty,
The land of the free, built on unity.

Next, the United Kingdom, the Union Jack waves,
A blend of St. George, St. Andrew, and St. Patrick's praise,
Red cross of England, white saltire of Scotland,
Red saltire of Ireland, a symbol of their bond.

A land of vast landscapes, Australia's flag unfurls,
A blue ensign with the Southern Cross, a constellation that whirls,
In green and gold, the Commonwealth Star,
A symbol of unity, stretching afar.

Canada's maple leaf, bold and red,
Echoes the nation's spirit, in its thread,
With two red bars on a white field,
A flag that represents values here revealed.

India's tricolour, saffron, white, and green,
Symbolises courage, peace, and tranquillity seen,
With a blue wheel, symbolising progress,
A flag that reflects the nation's success.

Japan's flag, a simple design,
A red disc on a white field, so fine,
The rising sun, a symbol of hope,
A nation's resilience, ready to cope.

Brazil's flag, a vibrant display,
A green field with a golden diamond array,
Within it, a blue sphere, stars shining bright,
Representing the states, a dazzling sight.

France's tricolour, blue, white, and red,
A symbol of liberty, and the bloodshed,
Equality and fraternity, values held dear,
A flag that represents, history clear.

Lesotho, be proud,
Your flag stands tall with honour and joy.
The stripes of blue and white do fly,
With the shield of your nation, high in the sky.
The sun and the Basotho hat stand bold,
Reminding us of the heritage we hold.

Israel, a land of faith and peace,
Your flag a symbol of hope to release.
A Star of David shines so bright,
With stripes of blue and white, such a sight.
Your land has seen so much pain and woe,
But your flag flies high with pride to show:
That you have overcome and stood so tall,
With strength and courage, you heard the call.
You stand united in faith and love,
A beacon of hope for us from above.

As we move across the globe's expanse,
Flags of nations, in a mesmerising dance,
Each unique, with meaning profound,
Representing cultures, forever renowned.

From Russia's tricolour to South Africa's rainbow,
From China's red flag to Mexico's eagle's glow,
Flags unite us, in diversity's embrace,
A testament to humanity's beautiful chase.

So let us celebrate, these symbols so grand,
Flags of nations, across every land,
They stand for unity, pride, and more,
A reminder of the nations we adore.

THE LIGHT OF THE SOUL

In a world filled with hustle and bustle,
Where worries and troubles often tussle,
There lies a treasure, oh so true,
A feeling that brings joy anew.

Happiness, like a gentle breeze,
Caresses hearts with tender ease,
It whispers it's melody soft and clear,
Wiping away every trace of fear.

From the first light of dawn till twilight's fall,
Happiness shimmers and covers all,
It dances merrily in every ray,
Painting skies in shades of gay.

Happiness is a child's laughter,
A melodious tune that echoes after,
A smile spreading across a face,
Like a warm and loving embrace.

It's the scent of rain on a summer's day,
Or a blooming flower in full array,
The taste of chocolate melting on your tongue,
Or the feeling of warmth when love is flung.

Happiness is found in a helping hand,
In heartfelt deeds that others understand,
A friend's touch when the world feels cold,
A peaceful moment, a story told.

It resides in the simplest of things,
Like the song a little songbird sings,
Or the comforting purr of a faithful pet,
Making worries and troubles forget.

Happiness is in a starlit sky,
Where dreams and hopes can freely fly,
It gleams in the eyes of those who share,
The joy and love they gladly bear.

It's the warmth that glows in a mother's smile,
The pride that shines in a father's guile,
The laughter shared by siblings near,
A bond unbroken, forever dear.

So seek happiness in every sunrise,
And in the twinkle of starlit skies,
For it's within reach, waiting for thee,
To embrace its joy, forever free.

Though life may bring its storms and strife,
Happiness is the beacon in this grand life,

So let it fill your days with cheer,
And let its light guide you far and near.

For happiness, my friend, is the key,
To unlock the doors of true ecstasy,
So hold it close within your heart,
And let it be your lifelong art.

THE DIPLOMATIC FOR HUMANITY

In a world of chaos and strife,
Embracing hope and changing lives,
Comes a leader, kind and wise,
António Guterres, a beacon in the skies.

Born in humble lands of Portugal's embrace,
From youth, his passion for justice would not erase,
Driven by empathy, love, and grace,
He aimed to make the world a better place.

With determination, he forged his way,
Through academia and political sway,
A man of substance, both night and day,
António Guterres, with a heart that won't betray.

He rose through ranks, his talents found,
A voice for the voiceless, standing proud,
Guided by principles, his compass sound,
Leading with integrity, as he treads the ground.

From refugees to climate change's toll,
António's vision seeks to make whole,
Lifting the vulnerable, healing the soul,

A champion for equality, making societies roll.

In halls of power, his words resound,
Calling for peace, where conflict is found,
Bridging divides, bringing nations around,
António Guterres, on common ground.

With diplomacy and eloquence, he speaks,
Tirelessly working, week after week,
Uniting countries, striving to seek,
Solutions for a world often bleak.

Through hurricanes and floods that drown,
In war-torn regions, where hope is gone,
António Guterres, with a compassionate crown,
Extends his hands to those forlorn.

In the face of adversity, he stands tall,
Empowering women, inspiring all,
Fighting injustice, answering the call,
António Guterres, our global curtain call.

So let us stand together, hand in hand,
Embrace the vision, the strength that he commands,
For a world united, where love expands,
António Guterres, leading with steadfast and grand.

In the legacy of this remarkable man,
Hope and humanity will forever span,
António Guterres, a visionary plan,
A symbol of progress, showing us we can.

THE BEAUTIFUL GAME

In stadiums filled with an electrifying crowd,
A beautiful game, both humble and proud,
Where heroes arise, with skill endowed,
Football, a passion that stands unbowed.

From dusty streets to grand arenas of acclaim,
Where dreams take flight, fueled by the game,
A symphony of feet, dancing with flame,
Football, a language that needs no name.

In grassroots clubs and childhood dreams,
A love affair with the ball, it seems,
Chasing destiny like flowing streams,
Football, a canvas for hope that gleams.

With every kick, the heartbeat quickens,
A rush of adrenaline, a moment that thickens,
The roar of the crowd, like thunder that sickens,
Football, a fairytale where hearts awaken.

From defenders with walls of might,
To strikers with speed and piercing sight,
Each position, a role to ignite,
Football, a tapestry woven in light.

Through rivalries fierce and battles fought,
Respect and honour, lessons taught,
Unity on the field, a bond well sought,
Football, a stage where legends are caught.

On green fields, dreams reach for the skies,
With every pass and goal that defies,
Inspiring hearts, igniting sighs,
Football, a spectacle that never dies.

From World Cups to leagues divine,
The magic of football, forever will shine,
Embracing cultures, crossing each line,
Football, a universal language so fine.

So let us gather, hands held as one,
In celebration of this game we've spun,
With joy and passion, together we've won,
Football, a symphony that can't be outdone.

In stadiums filled with an electrifying crowd,
A beautiful game, both humble and proud,
Where heroes arise, with skill endowed,
Football, our love, forever avowed.

WHY?

In life, we often wonder why,
Questions that make our spirits sigh.
Why is the sky so vast and blue?
Why do flowers blossom, so beautiful and true?

Why do the waves crash upon the shore?
Why does love leave us wanting more?
Why do tears fall from our eyes?
Why do we yearn for starry skies?

Why does the sun rise each morn?
Why do we dream?
Why do birds sing their melodies?
Why are there wars, destroying cities?

Why do we dream of what could be?
Why are we drawn to the endless sea?
Why do we hope when hope seems gone?
Why does time carry on and on?

Why does laughter heal our pain?
Why do memories sometimes wane?
Why do we ask these questions dear,
If answers aren't always clear?

For in the "why" we find our quest,
To seek, to learn, to do our best.
To understand life's mystery,
To find the meaning, to set it free.

The answers may elude our grasp,
But still, we strive, for truth we clasp.
For in the asking, we ignite,
A spark within, a guiding light.

So, let us ponder, question, explore,
The wonders of life, forevermore.
For in the "why" lies endless worth,
A quest that gives our lives a great birth.

THE SILENT HEALER

In the realm of dreams, where slumber prevails,
Lies a world so serene, where our mind unveils.
Sleep, oh sweet sleep, so gentle and deep,
A refuge for tired souls, a respite we seek.

In the silence of the night, as shadows dance,
Sleep wraps us tight in a blissful trance.
A surreal voyage to distant lands we'll take,
As the pillow embraces us, the world gently shakes.

Oh sleep, a sanctuary from life's daily strife,
To recharge our bodies and renew our life.
In the velvety darkness, where stars softly gleam,
We surrender ourselves to your peaceful stream.

As eyelids grow heavy, and thoughts start to fade,
Sleep guides us gently to a tranquil serenade.
A symphony of silence, calming and smooth,
As we wander through dreams, in the realm of truth.

Amidst the moonlit whispers, we drift away,
To a universe where worries can't hold sway.
The mind ventures free, where imagination plays,
In sleep's open arms, we wander and amaze.

Through fields of lavender and rivers of gold,
Sleep unveils a tapestry, wondrous to behold.
In dreams, we glimpse magic hidden from day,
Where fantasies flourish and doubts melt away.

The night becomes a canvas for dreams to create,
Fantastical stories, merging early and late.
In slumber's embrace, time begins to dissolve,
As we dance with the stars, and they silently revolve.

And when dawn breaks, and the night takes its leave,
We awaken refreshed, ready to believe,
That sleep, sweet sleep, a gift we receive,
To embrace each new day, with fervour and relief.

So cherish your slumber, embrace it with grace,
For sleep's tender touch can't be replaced.
In the depths of night, let dreams take flight,
And may peaceful sleep guide you through each night.
The adversary of all
In the realm of shadows, where mysteries dwell,
Lies a profound concept, a story to tell.
Death, oh solemn death, a part of life's course,
A journey we all take, with no final remorse.

In the tapestry of existence, a truth we must face,
That life's fleeting moments leave no trace.

Like petals that fall from a fragile flower,
Death reminds us of all of our limited hours.

Though sorrow may linger, and tears may well,
Death's embrace can weave a different spell.
For within its depths lie lessons untold,
A reminder of what it means to be bold.

In the face of mortality, we find clarity,
To cherish moments and live with sincerity.
To let go of grudges and nurture love's flame,
For in death's presence, all trivialities wane.

But death is not only a parting of ways,
It's a metamorphosis, a dance in the haze.
For life and death are intertwined,
Two sides of a coin, they'll forever bind.

In death, we find solace, a heavenly peace,
A chance for the spirit to find release.
Like the setting sun sinking into the night,
Death bestows upon us a luminous light.

And as we mourn, we celebrate life,
We honour the memories, through joy and strife.
For death is a reminder, to live with intent,
To savour each breath, to be truly present.

In the aftermath of loss, we find strength anew,
To carry the torch, and let our souls brew,
A legacy of love, resilience, and grace,
In honour of those who have found their resting place.

So let us not fear the inevitable end,
For death, our companion, helps us transcend.
In the tapestry of existence, it has its role,
A gentle reminder to embrace each soul.

For in the duality of life and death's embrace,
We find the beauty of the human race.
So let us live fully, with love as our guide,
As we navigate this journey, side by side.

THE LANGUAGE OF THE SOUL

In the realm of love, a wondrous terrain,
A tapestry of emotions, a heartfelt refrain,
There exist many types, as varied as can be,
Let me dive in, and help you see.

First, there's familial love, strong and pure,
A bond unbroken, forever secure,
From parents to siblings, a love so true,
Through thick and thin, they'll always see you through.

Then there's romantic love, a flame aflame,
Two souls entwined, sharing a name,
Passion ignites, in hearts that yearn,
Love's sweet dance, as the world turns.

Friendship blooms, another love so grand,
A companion in life, a helping hand,
Through laughter and tears, friendships grow,
Lifting spirits high, through highs and lows.

Self-love, a love often overlooked,
Nurturing oneself, feeling self-hooked,
For without love for oneself first and foremost,

Our love for others would be at its lowest.

Unconditional love, a love so rare,
No strings attached, no mask to wear,
A love that accepts, embraces flaws,
A love that uplifts, without any pause.

There's passionate love, filled with desire,
A fire that burns, unable to tire,
Intensity and fervour, hearts ablaze,
A love that consumes, in many ways.

Companionate love, a kind so calm,
A deep connection, a soothing balm,
Where friendship and affection intertwine,
A love that withstands the test of time.

Spiritual love, a love that transcends,
Connecting souls, where the divine extends,
A love for God, nature, or the universe,
Filling hearts with peace, comforting and diverse.

Puppy love, a young love so sweet,
Innocence and charm, a youthful beat,
Exploring feelings for the very first time,
A love that's tender, in its early prime.

Unrequited love, a bittersweet plight,
Feeling love's ache, in day and night,
Longing for someone, who's out of reach,
Yet cherishing the love, those words can't preach.

Love for humanity, in its grand scale,
A love that sees no borders, no land to trail,
A love that embraces, all colours and creeds,
A love that unites, fulfilling collective needs.

Maternal love, a love that's divine,
A mother's bond, forever in line,
Nurturing, protecting, with endless care,
A love that's unconditional, always there.

Paternal love, a father's embrace,
Guiding with strength, and steady grace,
A protector, a pillar, a guiding light,
A love that leads, both day and night.

Love for animals, a kindness so true,
A bond with creatures, that brings joy through,
A love that extends beyond our own kind,
Caring for those, with no voice to find.

In this vast spectrum of love's grand show,
Each type bears importance, that we must know,

For love is the essence, that makes us whole,
A universal language, to touch every soul.

So cherish the love, in all its form,
For it weathers life's storms, both cold and warm,
Let love be our anthem, shining so bright,
Guiding us forward, in love's eternal light.

THE FABRIC OF IDENTITY

The Fabric of Identity

In a world diverse, where nations unite,
Flags fly high, a symbol of their might,
Colours and emblems, waving in the air,
The pride of nations, to all who dare to stare.

Let's begin with the United States of America,
Old Glory's stars and stripes, a sight to remember,
Red, white, and blue, a beacon of liberty,
The land of the free, built on unity.

Next, the United Kingdom, the Union Jack waves,
A blend of St. George, St. Andrew, and St. Patrick's praise,
Red cross of England, white saltire of Scotland,
Red saltire of Ireland, a symbol of their bond.

A land of vast landscapes, Australia's flag unfurls,
A blue ensign with the Southern Cross, a constellation that whirls,
In green and gold, the Commonwealth Star,
A symbol of unity, stretching afar.

Canada's maple leaf, bold and red,
Echoes the nation's spirit, in its thread,
With two red bars on a white field,

A flag that represents values here revealed.

India's tricolour, saffron, white, and green,
Symbolises courage, peace, and tranquillity seen,
With a blue wheel, symbolising progress,
A flag that reflects the nation's success.

Japan's flag, a simple design,
A red disc on a white field, so fine,
The rising sun, a symbol of hope,
A nation's resilience, ready to cope.

Brazil's flag, a vibrant display,
A green field with a golden diamond array,
Within it, a blue sphere, stars shining bright,
Representing the states, a dazzling sight.

France's tricolour, blue, white, and red,
A symbol of liberty, and the bloodshed,
Equality and fraternity, values held dear,
A flag that represents, history clear.

Lesotho, be proud,
Your flag stands tall with honour and joy.
The stripes of blue and white do fly,
With the shield of your nation, high in the sky.
The sun and the Basotho hat stand bold,

Reminding us of the heritage we hold.

Israel, a land of faith and peace,
Your flag a symbol of hope to release.
A Star of David shines so bright,
With stripes of blue and white, such a sight.
Your land has seen so much pain and woe,
But your flag flies high with pride to show:
That you have overcome and stood so tall,
With strength and courage, you heard the call.
You stand united in faith and love,
A beacon of hope for us from above.

As we move across the globe's expanse,
Flags of nations, in a mesmerising dance,
Each unique, with meaning profound,
Representing cultures, forever renowned.

From Russia's tricolour to South Africa's rainbow,
From China's red flag to Mexico's eagle's glow,
Flags unite us, in diversity's embrace,
A testament to humanity's beautiful chase.

So let us celebrate, these symbols so grand,
Flags of nations, across every land,
They stand for unity, pride, and more,

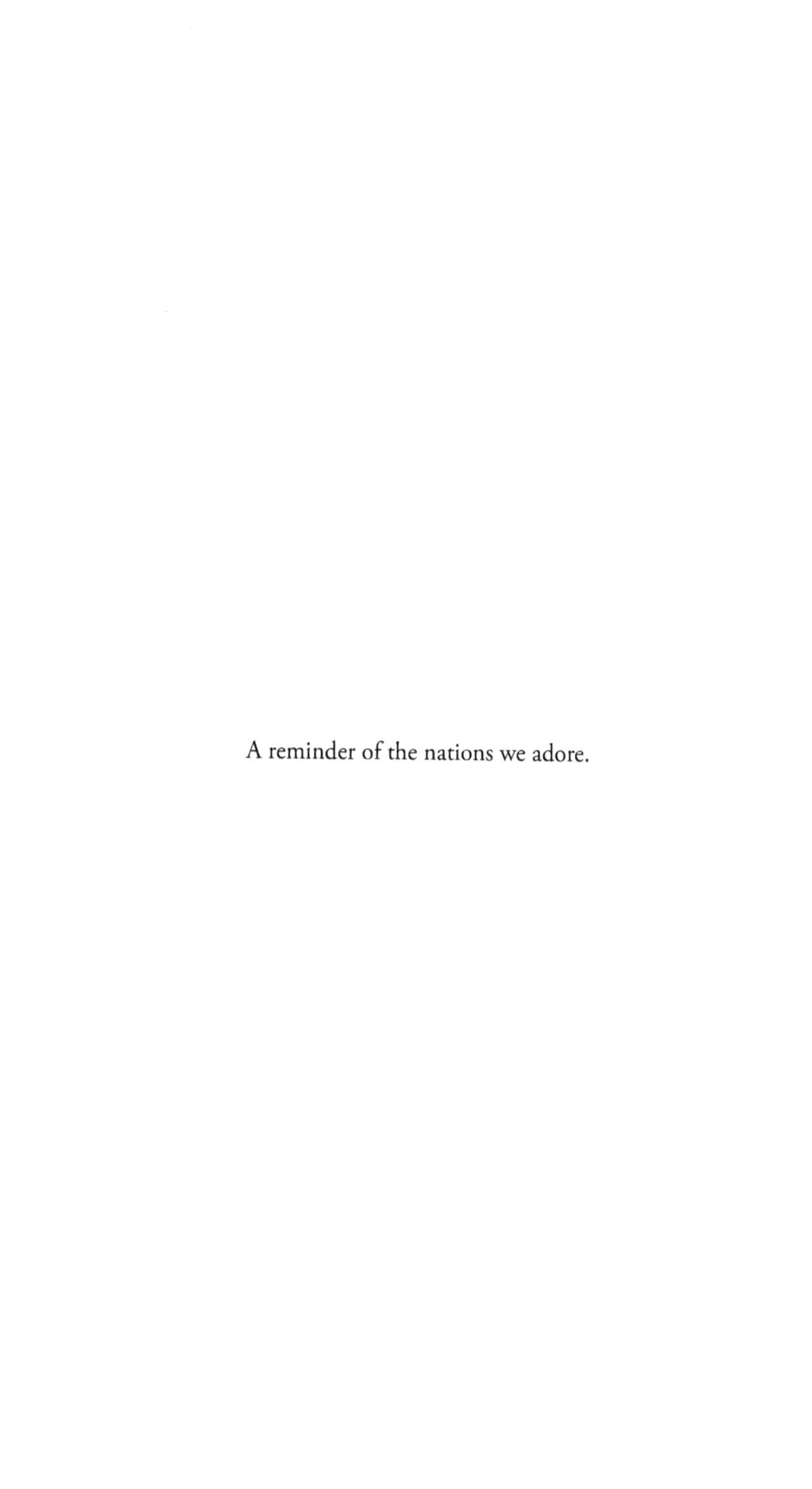

A reminder of the nations we adore.

THE ETERNAL FLOW

The Eternal Flow

In a land of green and blue, where nature's wonders thrive,
There flows a mighty river, with stories to revive.
Its waters gentle, yet fierce they run,
A timeless journey, under the golden sun.

Oh, river, how you wander with grace,
Carving paths through valleys, leaving no trace.
From lofty mountains, you are born,
A humble stream, through meadows adorned.

Splashing and dancing, you race along,
Singing a melody, a joyful song.
Through bustling towns and peaceful farms,
Nourishing life with your open arms.

Majestic trees lean towards your embrace,
Their branches caressed by your gentle chase.
Reflections shimmer upon your surface,
Mirroring a world, tranquil and flawless.

Creatures of all shapes and sizes find solace in your stream,
The timid deer, the soaring hawk, fulfils their wildest dream.
Fish swim in harmony beneath your shimmering sheen,

Birds serenade on your banks, their voices serene.

You carry the memories of ages past,
Of ancient civilizations whose reigns didn't last.
You've witnessed battles of great might,
And heard the whispers of love in the night.

With each passing bend, a new tale unfolds,
Of adventures undertaken, of treasures untold.
Captivating landscapes paint your shores,
A tapestry of colours that forever endures.

Oh, river, a symbol of life and change,
Constantly evolving, flowing no matter how strange.
You teach the lesson of going with the flow,
Accepting what comes, letting nature's rhythm show.

As the sun sets and the moon takes flight,
You continue your journey, guided by the night.
Restless yet peaceful, always moving ahead,
For that's the nature of a river, it is said.

So, let us cherish you, grand river of might,
For you hold secrets that illuminate the night.
A source of life, a witness to history,
Forever flowing, a symbol of mystery.

THE ART OF THE POSSIBLE

In the realm of politics, a complex game,
Where power and ideals intertwine, they claim.
Let me weave a tale, in verses sincere,
Using simple English, so all may hear.

Once upon a time, in a land of the free,
A nation thrived, called Democracy.
People gathered, with voices so strong,
To elect their leaders, to right the wrongs.

But alas, as time went by, divisions grew,
Politics transformed into battles anew.
Parties clashed, with differing views,
Ideas tossed around, like ships without crews.

Corruption crept in, like a silent thief,
Promises broken, causing much grief.
People yearned for honesty, for a true guide,
Someone who'd lead with integrity and pride.

Election day arrived, hope filled the air,
As candidates spoke, with passion and flair.
Citizens lined up, casting their vote,
Hoping for change, to set a new quote.

The winner emerged, with a triumph so grand,
A leader selected to take a firm stand.
But power can change, even the best heart,
As politics' influence tears virtues apart.

Laws were passed, with consequences unforeseen,
Some benefited, while others grew keen.
The rich got richer, the poor more burdened,
Struggles continued, hope seemingly hidden.

Yet amidst the chaos, a few champions stood,
Speaking for the weak, defending the good.
Voices like thunder, they rose above,
Fighting for justice, with courage and love.

Debates raged on, within crowded halls,
Issues discussed, as the nation called.
But in the midst of words, both sharp and kind,
Compromise seemed so hard to find.

Scandals erupted, shaking the land,
Trust eroding, like grains of sand.
Promises made, now broken and crushed,
The people's faith wavered, their dreams hushed.

But let us not forget, amidst this strife,
The power we hold, to shape our own life.

For politics, though complex and vast,
Relies on our voices, to make it last.

So let us stand together, hand in hand,
Demanding transparency, across the land.
In this political dance, we all have a role,
To heal the divides, and make us whole.

For in the end, politics is not just a game,
It's the foundation on which our society came.
So let us navigate these murky waters with care,
Using simple English, let's build a nation fair.

THE BLUE JEWEL OF THE COSMOS

Oh, Earth, our precious home so grand,
A place of wonder, vast and grand.
With landscapes diverse, and oceans wide,
You hold such beauty, nowhere to hide.

From towering mountains, reaching the skies,
To rolling hills, where nature lies.
Lush green forests, a symphony of trees,
Whispering secrets in the gentle breeze.

Oh, Earth, you provide, abundantly so,
Endless resources that we've come to know.
From fertile soils, where life takes root,
To rivers and lakes, an endless pursuit.

Your oceans, deep and teeming with life,
Mysteries hidden beneath the surface, rife.
An ecosystem diverse, thriving and strong,
A delicate balance, we mustn't do wrong.

From the smallest creatures, to the mighty beasts,
Within your embrace, each life finds its feast.
The fluttering wings of the colourful birds,

The graceful swim of the majestic herds.

Oh, Earth, you are the cradle of life,
Where countless species thrive, despite the strife.
Each creature unique, with a story to tell,
In the intricate tapestry where they dwell.

From the scorching deserts, where sunsets ignite,
To the icy poles, where frigid winds bite,
You offer extremes in climatic arrays,
A testament of your vastness, always in praise.

Yet, dear Earth, we must reflect upon our deeds,
For we hold the power to sow both flowers and weeds.
With careless actions, we've caused you harm,
Pollution and destruction, causing alarm.

But fear not, Earth, for there's hope still,
If we unite and embrace goodwill.
To nurture and protect, with love and care,
Preserving your wonders, for all to share.

For you are our home, the only place we know,
With your vibrant ecosystems, aglow.
Oh, Earth, let us stand as guardians true,
For the beauty and blessings bestowed by you.

So, let us cherish this precious sphere,
Protect its oceans, lands, and atmosphere.
With every step, let's tread with grace,
Embracing sustainability for every race.

Oh, Earth, our sanctuary, forever you'll be,
A testament to life's grand tapestry.
In your embrace, we find our worth,
Forever grateful for our home, the Earth.

PIECE OF WISDOM

Do not wait for tomorrow, what you can do today
A simple piece of wisdom, that can guide your way
For time is fleeting, and the days slip by
So make the most of every moment, don't let them pass you by

Each day is a gift, a chance to start anew
To follow your dreams, and make them come true
So don't waste a second, don't hesitate or stall
Seize the day and make the most of it all

Life is short, and it can be bittersweet
So cherish each moment, and make them all complete
Don't dwell on the past, or worry about the future
Live in the present, and let your light shine brighter

The power is within you, to make the most of every day
To live without regrets, and pave your own way
So don't wait for tomorrow, what you can do today
For this simple piece of wisdom, can guide you on your way

IS WORLD UNION POSSIBLE?

Will the world ever be united again,
In a symphony that erases the pain?
Where hearts beat together, in harmony's reign,
And peace resonates beyond borders and terrain.

Oh, how the world yearns for unity's embrace,
To erase division's mark and find a common space.
In a tapestry woven by hands of various race,
Each thread brings hope, for unity to embrace.

Gone are the days when we marvelled at our divide,
Now we hunger for unity, to stand side by side.
For in the bonds of togetherness, we confide,
That the world can heal, if we choose to abide.

In our shared struggles, we find strength anew,
And in compassion's embrace, dreams come true.
For unity lies not in what we pursue,
But rather in what we're willing to do.

Let us unite in the face of hatred's gleam,
And shatter the walls that intervene.
For when we recognize the humanity in each being,

A united world is no longer just a dream.

Can we mend the rifts that years did amass?
Sow love in hearts, where divisions trespass.
Perhaps within the whispers of empathy's class,
Lies the key to a world united at last.

Let us traverse the boundaries drawn by fear,
For unity's call is what we need to hear.
In the language of love, let us speak loud and clear,
Amidst the chaos, let kindness persevere.

We may stumble, we may falter, along this road,
But persevering forward, our strength bestowed.
For the hope of unity cannot be erode,
Together we stand, through tears and untold.

Oh, will the world ever be united again?
A question that resonates deep within.
But with every act of love, be it small or grand,
We reclaim unity, hand in hand.

So, let us continue to strive and to rise,
With kindness as our compass, we harmonise.
The world can be united again, we realise,
When love guides our actions, and compassion magnifies.

No matter the challenges that we may face,
Let unity be our mantra, in every place.
For within the hearts of humanity's embrace,
The world can be united, in peaceful grace.

WINTERS

In the land of winter's embrace, where snowflakes dance,
A season of wonder and enchanting trance.
The world is dressed in a blanket of white,
As the frosty air fills hearts with delight.

As the days grow shorter, and the nights grow long,
Winter's chill whispers a mesmerising song.
The trees stand tall, bare branches reaching high,
Their elegance silhouetted against the sky.

With every step, a soft crunch underfoot,
As snowflakes twinkle, delicate and mute.
Children bundled up, their laughter fills the air,
Building snowmen with great care and flair.

The birds migrate south, seeking warmer climes,
Leaving behind scenery painted in snow's rhymes.
Yet, some brave souls remain, in the cold they roam,
Their feathers fluffy, braving winter's home.

Jack Frost paints intricate patterns on the glass,
Transforming windows into a shimmering mass.
Ice crystals form, creating a spectacle divine,
A window into nature's captivating design.

Inside cosy homes, hearth fires glow,
Casting a warm and comforting glow.
Families gather around, laughter fills the space,
Sharing stories and love, finding solace and grace.

Hot cocoa warms hands, with marshmallows to stir,
As icy winds howl outside, a comforting purr.
Snug in blankets, lost in books or dreams,
Winter wraps hearts in its comforting schemes.

In winter's depths, the snowfall we adore,
A canvas for dreams, where memories endure.
Each flake unique, a miniature work of art,
Bathing the world in a tranquil winter's start.

Snowball fights and sledding down hillsides steep,
Immersed in joy, within winters' keep.
Snow angels grace the ground, wings spread wide,
Leaving imprints of innocence outside.

The silence of the world, under snow's embrace,
A hushed whisper, tranquil and full of grace.
A gentle reminder to slow down and ponder,
Reflecting on life, and the miracles we wander.

The beauty of winter lies not just in the snow,
But in the respite it brings from life's ebb and flow.

A season of rejuvenation, a time to restart,
A chance to find stillness, and listen to your heart.

When winter bids farewell, spring will arise,
Bringing forth new life, under sunlit skies.
But as we say goodbye, to winter's magical reign,
We'll forever cherish its beauty, in our hearts it'll remain.

So, let us embrace the season's frosty display,
For winter has its own enchanting way.
In chilly days and nights, snow gently falling,
It's a reminder of nature's wonders, enthralling.

SNOWFLAKES DESOLATION

Snowflakes desolation

When summer arrives with its golden hue,
The world awakens, vibrant and anew.
The sun shines brightly, casting its light,
Illuminating days, banishing the night.

The air hums with an electric thrill,
As nature's symphony sings with skill.
Leaves rustle in the warm, gentle breeze,
As flowers bloom with graceful ease.

The meadows are alive, a kaleidoscope of hues,
Butterflies flutter, a dance they infuse.
Birds serenade with their melodious tunes,
Underneath glorious summer moons.

Children's laughter fills the air,
As they run and play without a care.
Friends gather, side by side,
Seeking adventures far and wide.

The beaches beckon with their sandy shore,
Where waves crash and seagulls soar.
The salty scent of the ocean's embrace,
Invigorates the spirit, leaving no trace.

With each breath, the aroma of summer blooms,
Jasmine, roses, and sweet perfumes.
The trees provide shade, a cool retreat,
To escape the heat, finding solace sweet.

Picnics unfold on chequered blankets spread,
As families gather, breaking bread.
Juicy watermelons and berries so sweet,
A feast of flavours to truly beat.

Ice cream trucks roam the neighbourhoods,
Delighting tastebuds with sugary goods.
From chocolate to vanilla, to flavours rare,
A frozen treat to satisfy and share.

Crickets chirp in the balmy night,
Fireflies twinkle, radiant and bright.
Stargazers lay on blankets, eyes to the sky,
Witnessing constellations sail on by.

Summertime storms may arrive with a roar,
Lighting up the sky, thunder's encore.

Raindrops nourish the earth's thirsty ground,
Creating a symphony, nature's sound.

From summer camps to road trips long,
Adventure calls to those who dare belong.
Exploring mountains, forests, and streams,
Embracing nature, fulfilling dreams.

Festivals and fairs fill the summer air,
With vibrant colours and music to bear.
Savouring cotton candy and fairground delights,
Creating memories that reach new heights.

As summer draws to a bittersweet end,
Memories of warmth and joy surely send.
The days grow shorter, but hearts remain,
Filled with the echoes of summer's reign.

So, let us cherish the season's embrace,
Embrace the sunshine on our face.
For summer is a time to live and explore,
A reminder of all that life has in store.

In the laughter of children and the scent of flowers,
In adventures and moments that last for hours,
Summer weaves its magic, weaving dreams,
Enveloping all in its sun-kissed beams.

So, as summer unfurls, embrace its grace,
Find joy in each moment, at your own pace.
For summer is a reminder of life's sweet refrain,
Where memories are made and dreams attain.

VERSIFICATORS

Versificators

In the realm of words, where emotions take flight,
In the hearts of dreamers, poets find their might.
With pen in hand, and thoughts that ignite,
They weave tapestries of beauty, against the night.

Poets, the painters of the soul's landscape,
Capturing emotions, both joy and heartache.
They dance with words, like stars in the sky,
Creating symphonies that touch hearts, oh so high.

In the depths of their thoughts, they find solace,
Expressing the human experience, beyond any malice.
They craft verses, like whispers in the wind,
Revealing truths that lie within.

With delicate strokes, they paint longing and desire,
Their words alight, in passionate pyres.
They unravel mysteries, hidden deep within,
Delighting readers, letting imaginations spin.

In verses, they conjure worlds, both real and surreal,
A realm of imagination, where dreams are revealed.
With each line, they construct a new reality,

Where readers find refuge, and souls find clarity.

The poet's mind, a kaleidoscope of thoughts,
A conduit for emotions, all tangled in knots.
They dive into the abyss, fearlessly exploring,
Questioning existence, a ceaseless soaring.

With empathy's embrace, they traverse lives,
Stepping into others' shoes, where compassion thrives.
They shed light on injustices, and societal ills,
Their words are a beacon, for hearts that want to heal.

Poetry, a language that defies the mundane,
The poets' craft, dancing in rhythmic refrain.
They play with metaphors and similes, with delight,
Finding beauty in darkness, and shining it bright.

They capture moments, like photographs in time,
Freezing emotions, forever sublime.
Their words carry echoes of past and present,
Leaving a legacy, in hearts imprinted.

But as poets venture in the realms of prose,
They often feel like outsiders, in a world that seldom knows.
Yet their words penetrate, hearts open wide,
For poetry has a way of breaking down divides.

So, let us celebrate the poets' rhymes,
For they reveal truths, beyond the confines.
In simple words, they ignite a fire,
Sparking change and inspiring hearts to aspire.

In solitude or among a crowd,
Poets emerge, their voices unbowed.
They offer solace, in times of despair,
For their words show that someone out there cares.

To the poets who paint with words so fine,
Whose verses dance to the rhythm of time,
We thank you for your art, your soul's unveiling,
For through your words, the world keeps unveiling.

Poets, the wanderers of the soul's expanse,
Guiding us through life's intricate dance.
Through you we find solace, through you we find grace,
Poets, your words illuminate this human race.

ARE LEADERS MADE OR BORN?

Are leaders made or born? A question oft debated,
In the realm of influence, where destinies are fated.
Do they step onto the stage, with innate skill and might,
Or do they mould their abilities, through persistence and insight?

Some say leaders are born, with qualities ingrained,
Inherent traits and charisma, that cannot be trained.
They possess a natural presence, a magnetic allure,
Inspiring others effortlessly, with words that endure.

But others argue, that leaders are made through time,
Through experiences and challenges, their character does climb.
They learn from failures, and rise above strife,
Developing the resilience to navigate life.

Leaders gain wisdom, through lessons they embrace,
They master the art of adaptability and grace.
They seek knowledge, with an insatiable thirst,
Absorbing wisdom, from the best and the worst.

In the crucible of circumstances, leaders emerge,
Through hardships faced, their resilience surges.
They learn to communicate, to listen and to speak,

Harnessing the power to inspire and critique.

Leaders are made, some voices proclaimed,
Through dedication to growth, they transcend mere acclaim.
They hone their skills, with unwavering devotion,
Striving for excellence, with unwavering motion.

Yet, in this debate, perhaps truth lies between,
A blend of nature and nurture, in this leadership scene.
For while some may possess natural gifts, a head start,
It is the journey of growth that defines the leader's heart.

Leaders may be born, with innate qualities rare,
But it is their choices and actions that truly declare.
Their resolve and determination, through trials they face,
That sculpt their leadership, leaving an indelible trace.

So, let not the debate divide us, or cast us apart,
For leaders can be made, and leaders can start,
With a spark within, and a willingness to grow,
They can step into greatness, their influence to bestow.

Leaders are made, and so they shall be,
Through learning and growth, a constant decree.
With open minds and hearts, they forge ahead,
Influencing others, where their footprints are spread.

Let us celebrate leaders, both born and made,
For they shape our world, with decisions they've laid.
May they inspire us all, to reach our own potential,
To lead with integrity, and a spirit transcendental.

For leaders, born or made, lead us with might,
Illuminating paths, in the darkness of night.
They guide and inspire, through their actions bold,
Creating a legacy, that in our hearts forever holds.

PEACE

In a world filled with endless strife and pain,
Yearning for harmony, we seek to attain,
A tranquil oasis, where hearts are at rest,
A soothing balm for souls, a true peace bequest.

Oh, peace, elusive yet noble, we crave thee,
In every corner of life, let your light be,
From towering mountains to the vast expanse,
Unite humanity, let peace enhance.

Let peace blossom like flowers in spring's embrace,
Resplendent petals swaying with gentle grace,
Each petal a symbol, a prayer for deep calm,
Together, let's weave a harmonious psalm.

Peace, like a hummingbird's delicate flight,
Has the power to overcome the darkest night,
With its wings of compassion, it spreads its charm,
Healing wounds, erasing hatred's alarm.

Imagine a river, serene and clear,
Winding through hearts, wiping away each tear,
Its gentle current carries away all strife,
Uniting souls, bringing harmony to life.

Let's cast aside weapons and embrace a dove,
For violence only breeds hearts devoid of love,
Peace is the beacon that guides us from despair,
Illuminating paths with tender care.

Look to the sky, where the stars brightly gleam,
Their celestial dance, a celestial dream,
Each twinkle reminds us of hope untold,
That peace can reign supreme, its power unfolds.

In the embrace of peace, let us find solace,
Where prejudice and hatred have no place,
Embracing differences, with open arms wide,
For peace knows no boundaries, no divide.

Let kindness be our guide, our compass true,
For in kindness, peace will surely ensue,
Speak with words of love, rather than of war,
Let peace be our language, now and forevermore.

Though the world may tremble, as uncertainties grow,
With peace as our anchor, we shall weather the blow,
Together, hand in hand, we shall endure,
For peace's triumph is steadfast and pure.

Oh, peace, embrace us in your gentle sway,
Banishing darkness, bringing a brand-new day,

With unity and love, may we finally cease,

And find everlasting solace in true peace.

PINNACLES OF PROGRESS

In a bustling city, where dreams aspire high,
Air scrapers pierce the sky, reaching for the night,
Towering giants, with glass and steel embraced,
They define our skyline, in this urban space.

Oh, air scrapers, rising tall, touching the clouds,
Like sentinels they stand, attracting crowds,
Their gleaming windows reflect the sun's glow,
A modern marvel, a sight to behold.

From bottom to top, they stretch to extreme heights,
A testament to human achievement's might,
Each floor a habitat for work and for play,
Where dreams come alive, shaping the urban fray.

The concrete and metal, a symphony of might,
Constructed with precision, reaching for light,
They scrape the very air, defying all bounds,
Creating a metropolis where vision resounds.

These vertical marvels, they shape our skyline,
A beacon of progress, a place to divine,
Within their towering walls, the world merges,
Bringing together cultures, blending all urges.

From ground zero, we look up in awe,
At the might and majesty of what we saw,
Each floor a story, each level a tale,
Where aspirations thrive, never to fail.

But amidst the grandeur, let not nature fade,
In this concrete jungle, let's find a new trade,
Intertwined with the air scrapers, let greenery grow,
Creating harmony, a balance to bestow.

In their towering stature, let's find grace,
A reminder of nature's profound embrace,
For even in the midst of concrete and steel,
We can find solace and a love we can feel.

So, as the air scrapers soar towards the sky,
Let's seek to find a balance, let's not deny,
That progress and nature can coexist,
In a world where harmony and beauty persist.

In the shadow of air scrapers, let's pause and see,
The intersection of dreams and tranquillity,
For even amidst the hustle and the noise,
We can find moments of peace and joyful poise.

Oh, air scrapers, symbols of human might,
May you inspire us to reach for new heights,

But let us never forget the beauty that surrounds,

In this vast world, where peace and love resounds.

SEASON OF HOPE

The season of joy, the time of yuletide cheer,
As Christmas approached, anticipation drew near,
The world adorned in lights, shimmering and bright,
Preparing for the festivities that would last through the night.

In homes and in hearts, the Christmas spirit did flow,
As children's laughter echoed, like a gentle winter snow,
Decorations adorned every corner and nook,
Bringing warmth and wonder with every loving look.

The Christmas tree stood tall, its branches spread wide,
With ornaments and tinsel, twinkling with pride,
A symbol of hope, evergreen and true,
Reminding us of love and blessings anew.

Families gathered 'round, for a festive feast,
Roasted turkey, warm pies, each plate a delicious beast,
Laughter filled the air, as stories were shared,
Creating memories that would forever be cherished and cared for.

Carols filled the streets, sung with joy and elation,
Spreading melodies of peace and pure adoration,
Children's voices soared, reaching heights on high,
Singing of the baby, born under a starlit sky.

Gifts were exchanged, with hearts full of glee,
A gesture of love, a symbol of unity,
Wrapped with care, adorned with bows,
Expressing gratitude, more than words could disclose.

The fireplace crackled, as warmth filled the room,
Creating a cosy ambiance, dispelling any gloom,
Embracing loved ones, in hugs of pure delight,
Basking in the love that made the season bright.

Beyond the material, the true meaning shone,
A celebration of faith, a love that's known,
The birth of a saviour, a guiding star so bright,
Bringing hope to the world, with its heavenly light.

For Christmas is a time of compassion and giving,
A season that reminds us of the art of forgiving,
Of spreading kindness and goodwill throughout,
Filling hearts with love and casting away doubt.

So let us rejoice, as Christmas gathers near,
Embracing the spirit, without any fear,
With love in our hearts and joy in our souls,
May this Christmas season bring us closer, make us whole.

In the magic of Christmas, may we find peace,
May troubles cease, and all worries cease,

For as we come together, hand in hand,
We illuminate the world, like the brightest strand.

And as the snow gently falls, creating a serene sight,
We celebrate Christmas, with hearts filled with light,
Spreading love and hope, like the glittering snow,
May the joy of this season continue to grow.

THE FESTIVAL OF LIGHT

In a land vibrant and rich, where traditions abound,
India prepares for a festival renowned,
Diwali, the festival of lights, brings joy far and wide,
A celebration of triumph, where darkness must hide.

In every nook and corner, lamps are aglow,
Guiding the way, casting a radiant show,
From the humblest homes to the grandest abodes,
The sparkle of diyas lights up the roads.

With anticipation mounting, preparations begin,
Cleaning and decorating, to welcome goodness in,
Rangolis adorn the floors, with intricate design,
A colourful welcome, both elegant and fine.

Sweets and savouries are prepared with care,
A feast fit for gods, the aroma fills the air,
From laddoos to barfis, a delightful array,
Shared with loved ones, on this auspicious day.

New clothes, sparkling and bright, are donned with pride,
Symbolising the fresh start, a journey beside,
Families gather, hearts full of love,
Seeking blessings, from the heavens above.

Fireworks light up the sky, bursting with cheer,
Crackling and sparkling, bringing magic near,
As they illuminate the night, their colours dance,
Filling hearts with delight, a joyous trance.

But Diwali is more than just lights in the sky,
It's a tale of triumph, of good overcoming the sly,
With the return of Lord Rama, prince of great renown,
Diwali commemorates his victory, casting darkness down.

On this day, we remember and honour the fight,
The triumph of good over evil, shining so bright,
Let the light of Diwali guide us on our way,
Illuminating the path, dispelling shadows each day.

But amidst the celebrations, let's not forget,
The spirit of unity, a bond we must protect,
Come together, embrace all, with hearts open wide,
Spreading love and harmony, with no divide.

Reach out to those in need, extend a helping hand,
For in Diwali's glow, let compassion expand,
Let's fill the lives of others with hope and cheer,
Lighting up their hearts, spreading joy near and dear.

So as the festivities come to an end,
Let the spirit of Diwali forever extend,

May the light within us continue to shine,
In every step we take, in every moment divine.

Diwali, a celebration of light and love,
A reminder of blessings, bestowed from above,
As joy fills the air and hearts are aglow,
India celebrates, letting the Diwali spirit grow.

THE STAR OF ASIA

In Patiala, a place of cultural zest,
Stands proudly Punjabi University, one of the best,
Nestled in green fields, a haven serene,
Where knowledge is nurtured, a vibrant dream.

With its majestic campus, grand and wide,
Punjabi University fills hearts with pride,
A haven of education, where students dwell,
Seeking wisdom's treasures, as stories they tell.

From the towering buildings to the sprawling lawns,
Every corner whispers tales of knowledge spawns,
Lecture halls echo with eager minds,
As teachers guide, wisdom enshrined.

Under the shade of ancient trees so tall,
Students gather, laugh and play, one and all,
With camaraderie and friendship so strong,
Memories are woven, forever lifelong.

The library, a treasure trove of books so vast,
Inviting exploration into the realms of the past,
Where pages turn with intellectual delight,
Igniting passions, igniting the mind's flight.

Academic prowess resonates in every course,
Covering arts, sciences, and even discourse,
From languages to technology's call,
Punjabi University caters to one and all.

But it's more than just the learning inside,
It's the spirit of Punjabi, bursting with pride,
Celebrations bloom, festivals take flight,
Embracing traditions, day and night.

Bhangra fills the air, with lively beats,
Dazzling performances, enchanting feats,
Giddha dancers twirl, with grace and flair,
The Punjabi spirit, vibrant and rare.

Sports fields come alive, as athletes compete,
With passion and dedication, they never retreat,
Representing Punjabi University with might,
Their achievements shine, like stars in the night.

Punjabi University, a hub for cultural exchange,
Embracing diversity, beyond any range,
From Punjab's heart, it spreads its glory,
Weaving unity in India's grand tapestry.

And as the years go by, memories held dear,
Cherishing the moments spent here,

Punjabi University leaves an indelible mark,
Imparting wisdom, igniting sparks.

Patiala's gem, a beacon of higher learning,
With knowledge as its fire, forever burning,
Punjabi University stands tall and divine,
A symbol of excellence, a place so fine.

THE CONTINENT OF DIVERSITY

In Europe, oh so grand and wide
There's so much beauty to be spied
From the Eiffel Tower to the Colosseum's might
There's history and wonder at every sight

In Paris, the city of love and art
The Seine River flows, it's just a part
Of the grandeur and charm, oh so fair
The Louvre, Notre Dame, they're all there

In Rome, the ancient city so old
Where gladiators fought and stories were told
The ruins of the past still stand tall
Reminding us of history's call

In London, the city of fog and cheer
Big Ben chimes and the Thames flows clear
The red buses, black cabs, and royalty's grace
Have made this city a special place

In Athens, where democracy began
The Acropolis stands, a beacon to span
The centuries and remind us all

Of the birthplace of Western civilization's call

In Barcelona, with its Gaudi design
The Sagrada Familia, so divine
The art and culture, the tapas and more
Make this city a treasure to explore

From the Alps to the Mediterranean shore
Europe's landscapes leave you wanting more
The castles, the cathedrals, the cobblestone streets
The beauty of Europe simply can't be beat

So if you have the chance to roam
Through Europe, this diverse and welcoming home
Take in the sights, the sounds, the tastes
And savour the memories that you embrace

THE LAND OF OPPORTUNITY

In America, a land so vast and grand
From the Arctic wilds to the southern sand
A continent of diversity, so wide and free
From sea to shining sea, what wonders to see

In the north, Canada's forests lush and green
With lakes and mountains, a breathtaking scene
Majestic moose and grizzlies roam
A land of beauty, a natural home

In the south, the jungles of the Amazon
Teeming with life, a vibrant phenomenon
Mighty rivers flow, and the canopy's spread
A place so ancient, where time's been led

In Mexico, the land of ancient Mayan lore
Pyramids and temples, the ruins of yore
The colours, the flavours, the culture so rich
It's a land that bewitches, a bewitching hitch

In the United States, from sea to shining sea
Sweeping prairies, and mountains so free
Skyscrapers in the city, and wide-open plains

Filled with hopes and dreams, and endless gains

In Central America, the land of the Maya
Lush rainforests and volcanoes that
The vibrant culture, the traditions so dear
Central America, a land to hold near

In the Caribbean, the isles so fair
Turquoise waters, and warm, gentle air
White sandy beaches, and palm trees sway
A place of relaxation, where troubles wash away

So much to see and so much to do
In this continent, so grand and true
From the northern realms to the southern shore
America, a land to deeply adore

DRUG ABUSE

In the darkness of despair and pain
Lies a battle that drives many insane
A poison that grips with a deadly hold
Leaving shattered lives, stories untold

The lure of escape, the promise of bliss
But the road to addiction is paved with amiss
It starts with a high, a moment of ease
But soon it becomes a relentless disease

It tears families apart, and breaks hearts
Leaving behind a trail, of shattered parts
Once a solace becomes a heavy chain
As the grip of addiction slowly reigns

It preys on the lost, the broken, and weak
And steals away the futures they seek
The lifeblood it drains, and the dreams it devours
Leaving behind only ruins and hours

But hope still lingers in the darkest of night
A chance for recovery, a glimmer of light
With love and support, and a will to fight
The battles of addiction can be won in spite

So let's raise our voices and lend a hand
For those caught in the grip of this cruel demand
Let's break the chains, let's ease their pain
And restore the lives that were once so sane.

In the shadows, where despair takes root,
Lives are consumed by a poisonous pursuit.
The pills, the powders, the needle's sting,
Each choice leads to suffering.

Fleeting highs, a moment's respite,
But soon the addiction takes its bite.
The body aches, the mind screams,
In the relentless grip of drug-fueled dreams.

Families shattered, friendships strained,
As loved ones watch, feeling drained.
The lies, the theft, the endless need,
Leaving hearts broken, hearts that bleed.

The downward spiral, an endless descent,
As life becomes a cruel torment.
The promise of escape, a cruel delusion,
Leads to destruction and disillusion.

But in the depths, hope still resides,
A chance for healing, a change in tides.

With support and care, and a guiding hand,
Recovery begins, like grains of sand.

So let's reach out, let's break the chains,
And show that love and hope remains.
For those trapped in the clutches of despair,
A way out exists, we must all declare.

THE ELIMINATOR

In the hands of a man
A gun fears no one
It brings power and fear
A tool of destruction
A weapon of death

It's cold metal gleaming
Ready to unleash
Its deadly force
A force that can shatter
Lives and dreams

But in the wrong hands
It brings nothing but pain
Leaving behind
A trail of sorrow
And broken hearts

So let us handle it with care
And use it only when we must
For a gun is a double-edged sword
That can bring both
Life and death.
In the hands of a man

A gun commands attention
It demands respect
And changes the course of fate

With a pull of the trigger
It can silence a voice
Snuff out a flame
And leave a void in its wake

But in the quiet of the night
It can also protect
A guardian in the darkness
A shield against harm

Yet, the weight of its power
Should never be taken lightly
For a gun holds the power
To bring both
Hope and despair

So let us handle it with caution
And keep in mind its might
For a gun is a force to reckon with
That can mould our destiny
For better or for worse.

PANDORA'S BOX

In a world filled with fear,
Nuclear weapons loom near.
A deadly power in the wrong hands,
Can bring destruction to our lands.

The threat of war and devastation,
Lies within these weapons of annihilation.
A mushroom cloud, a blinding light,
Can wipe out cities in a single night.

The consequences of using such force,
Leaves the world without remorse.
The lives lost, the suffering endured,
Are the result of a power procured.

Let us strive for peace and understanding,
And work towards a future less demanding.
For in the end, it is our choice,
To silence the threat of the nuclear voice.

Let's come together and stand as one,
And ensure that this madness is finally done.
Let's dismantle these weapons, erase the threat,
And prevent a future that's filled with regret.

For a world free of nuclear strife,
Is a world where we can truly thrive.
Let's spread love and not the fear,
And make sure these weapons disappear.

It's time to choose a safer way,
And ensure that peace is here to stay.
Let's work towards a future that's bright,
And say goodbye to the nuclear night.

THE LAND OF ANCIENT WISDOM

In the heart of the East, Asia lies
From the towering Himalayas to the azure skies
A land of ancient culture and rich history
With diverse people and stunning scenery

From the bustling streets of Tokyo at dawn
To the tranquil temples of Angkor Wat at morn
Asia's tapestry is woven with vibrant hues
And a blend of traditions, old and new

China's Great Wall stands steadfast and strong
A testament to resilience that has lasted long
Japan's cherry blossoms paint the land in pink
While India's Taj Mahal makes lovers' hearts sink

Thailand's floating markets teem with life
And Indonesia's rice terraces cut like a knife
Through the lush green landscape, a sight to behold
Asia's wonders never fail to leave us awestruck and bold

The flavours of Asia tantalise the palate
From spicy curries to delicate dim sum, we savour
The aromas and tastes that dance on our tongues

A culinary journey that leaves us forever young

From the mighty Ganges to the Mekong's flow
Asia's rivers have stories to tell, secrets to show
And in its bustling cities, life never stops
In the midst of chaos, there's a rhythm that propels and docks

So let's celebrate the beauty of Asia's lands
The vibrant tapestry woven by diverse hands
From the mountains to the seas, and all in between
Asia's enchanting spirit will forever be seen.

THE GREAT DIVIDE

Today's generation
Drowns in technology
Always staring at screens
Never a moment of peace

Previous generations
Worked hard with their hands
Connected with nature
And cherished the simple things

Today's generation
Is constantly seeking validation
On social media platforms
Where likes and followers reign supreme

Previous generations
Found validation within
Their own achievements
And the love of family and friends

Today's generation
Seeks instant gratification
With everything at their fingertips
They struggle with patience and perseverance

Previous generations
Understood the value of hard work
And the satisfaction of earning
Their successes and accomplishments

Today's generation
Is filled with potential
But must not forget
The wisdom of their predecessors

For in blending the old and the new
They will find balance and strength
And pave the way for a future
That honours the best of both generations.

Today's generation
Is growing up in a world of fast-paced change
Where information flows at lightning speed
And the pressure to keep up is ever-present

But let us not forget
That previous generations
Faced their own struggles and hardships
And weathered their own storms

While today's generation
Lives in a world of instant communication

Previous generations
Knew the value of face-to-face interactions

Today's generation
Is passionate and vocal
About important social issues
And fighting for a better world

And yet, previous generations
Fought their own battles for change
With courage and determination
To leave behind a legacy of progress

So let us learn from each other
And not disregard the wisdom
That comes from the experiences
Of both today and yesterday's generations

For in understanding our differences
And embracing our similarities
We can create a brighter future
That honours the past and welcomes the future.

THE CELESTIAL WONDER

In the early morn, when darkness fades away,
A gentle glow emerges, welcoming the day.
The world awakens, as the sky turns bright,
A splendid scene unfolds, a breathtaking sight.

The sun peeks over the horizon's crest,
Painting the sky in colours, the very best.
Shades of pink and orange slowly unfurl,
As golden rays dance and twirl.

The birds begin to sing, their melodies sweet,
As nature rises up on its wondrous feet.
The world is filled with a golden haze,
A tranquil moment, it leaves us in a daze.

The sleepy land, now bathed in light,
Shadows recede, like creatures of the night.
Dewdrops on leaves sparkle and gleam,
In this divine moment, all is serene.

The sun, like a painter with its radiant brush,
Colours the world with a gentle hush.
Majestic mountains and rolling hills,
Valleys and meadows, adorned with thrills.

The warmth of the sunlight reaches the ground,
Embracing the earth all around.
It breathes life into flowers, trees, and streams,
Igniting their beauty, like magical dreams.

As morning progresses, the world comes alive,
With each passing moment, the day will thrive.
Gentle breezes carry scents of blooming flowers,
Whispering secrets through serene hours.

The sky transforms into a boundless blue,
As daylight treads, the past night bids adieu.
A brand-new day, a fresh start to embrace,
Embracing every moment, every trace.

So, rise with the sun, let its rays inspire,
Fill your heart with hope, let your spirit aspire.
For every sunrise holds a promise anew,
To live, to love, to make your dreams come true.

HOT CHOCOLATE

On a chilly day, when the wind blows cold
Nothing warms the heart like hot chocolate bold

A steaming cup, with marshmallows on top
Brings comfort and warmth that never will stop

It's like a hug from the inside out
Filling the soul with happiness, no doubt

The rich, creamy taste, oh so sweet
Makes every sip a delightful treat

So gather 'round, and savour the delight
Hot chocolate brings joy, day or night!
When the snow falls and the world turns white
Hot chocolate is the perfect respite

It's a cosy embrace in a cup
A soothing remedy when spirits are up

With its melt-in-your-mouth chocolatey bliss
There's nothing quite like it, no can't-miss

So let's raise our mugs and toast to this drink
That warms us through and makes us all think

Of the simple pleasures in life, so true
Hot chocolate, we're grateful for you.

I would like to thank all teachers who have inspired me over the years, both present and past, you will always be my teachers. With gratitude in my heart, I appreciate the support of my family, your encouragement means a world to me. A special thanks to notion press, who helped me shape this collection.

www.ingramcontent.com/pod-product-compliance
Lightning Source LLC
Chambersburg PA
CBHW021539150726
47990CB00006B/2309